When your child's
marriage ends

DIFFICULT TIMES SERIES

WHEN YOUR CHILD'S MARRIAGE ENDS

MILDRED TENGBOM

Augsburg Books
MINNEAPOLIS

WHEN YOUR CHILD'S MARRIAGE ENDS

Large-quantity purchases or custom editions of this book are available at a discount from the publisher. For more information, contact the sales department at Augsburg Fortress, Publishers, 1-800-328-4648, or write to: Sales Director, Augsburg Fortress, Publishers, P.O. Box 1209, Minneapolis, MN 55440-1209.

Scripture passages are from the New Revised Standard Version of the Bible, copyright © 1946, 1952, 1971, 1989 by the Division of Christian Education of the National Council of the Churches of Christ in the USA. Used by permission.

Cover design by David Meyer
Book design by Jessica A. Klein

Library of Congress Cataloging-in-Publication Data
Tengbom, Mildred.
  When your child's marriage ends / by Mildred Tengbom.
     p. cm.—(Difficult times series)
  ISBN 0-8066-4424-9 (alk. paper)
      1. Divorce—Psychological aspects. 2. Parent and adult child.
3. Grandparent and child. 4. Divorced people—Family relationships.
5. Loss (Psychology) I. Title. II. Series.
HQ814.T424 2002
306.89—dc21   2002074411

The paper used in this publication meets the minimum requirements of American National Standard for Information Sciences—Permanence of Paper for Printed Library Materials, ANSI Z329.48-1984. ♾™

Manufactured in the U.S.A.

06   05   04   03   02   1   2   3   4   5   6   7   8   9   10

∽ Contents ∽

First Words

Quite likely, you are holding this little book in your hands because a son or daughter is in the process of a divorce. You are feeling the anguish and long to help. My husband and I know what it is like. We've been there, too, and in one sense, we're still there. Sometimes we wonder if the pain will be with us the rest of our lives.

In writing this book, in order to get a broad perspective, I relied heavily on recently published articles in journals. The articles usually reported the results of studies. Some of the journals are: *Journal of Divorce, Generations, International Journal of Aging and Human Development, The Gerontologist, Journal of Gerontological Social Work, Journal of Divorce and Remarriage, Journal of Religion, Journal of Community Health Nursing,* and *Journal of Marriage and the Family.* In addition, I referred to some books, and probably more importantly, I conducted interviews with a number of parents. Some parents kindly filled out questionnaires I sent them. I also talked to a few divorcing couples and a few grandchildren. I am indebted to all these sources.

This little book is but a primer. I am sure you, along with my husband and me, will want to continue your search so healing and health can come to all members of our families. We long and pray for this. May God enable us.

∽ *Chapter One* ∽
What to Expect

Divorce Is a Process

The divorce of your child had its beginning a long time before your child told you she feared it was going to happen or before your son told you he had left his wife. Months, maybe years, of unhappiness had preceded the action. Maybe you knew nothing about this, or maybe you had been concerned but kept hoping for the best. Regardless, chances are the announcement has hit you in the middle of your stomach.

"I was devastated," one mother said. Shocked, angry, confused, afraid. These are some of the words parents have used to describe their first reaction. A few have said, "relieved" or "actually happy." Parents using these latter words likely have been aware of the abuse and mistreatment their daughter or son had been enduring for some time. But even in these cases the announcement brings a certain amount of fear, anxiety, worry, and, as is true in all cases, sadness.

Divorce Has Many Causes

Those who have studied families have noted that families go through periods of stability and transition. Marriage and births bond families together. During adolescence, midlife, and retirement, certain forces are at work to disconnect family members.

Why at these times? Because during these times personal wants, desires, and aspirations may take precedence over the good of the family.

Some couples learn to allow space for personal desires without it weakening the family structure. Some couples learn to sublimate personal desires and still find happiness. And some couples learn the art of give and take and season their daily lives well with forgiveness, and the family structure remains intact. Others do not know how to or do not choose to persevere in learning this.

There are as many reasons for rifts in relationships as there are people: discovery of incompatibility; personalities changing with the years; involvement in drugs, alcohol, or gambling; infidelity; impaired health with its demands—the list could go on and on.

DIVORCE IS EXPENSIVE

After the first declaration of intent, one of the spouses usually moves out of the home. The time of physical separation begins. This may last anywhere from a couple of months to two or three years.

The end of this stage occurs when one spouse files for legal separation or divorce. Occasionally, legal separation leads to reconciliation. More often it ends later in divorce proceedings.

Sometimes a couple may use one lawyer together. More commonly, each party hires a lawyer. Meetings with lawyers, discussions about division of property, child custody, and child support fill the weeks preceding the day in court.

Finally, the parties arrive at an agreement on all issues. The petitioner and respondent and their lawyers appear before a judge who asks a few questions. If the judge receives satisfactory answers, he then asks the petitioner if he or she wants the marriage dissolved. The petitioner responds, "Yes." The judge then says, "The marriage is dissolved." That marks the legal end to a union begun with joy and in high anticipation.

Procedures vary from state to state, but in general this is what takes place.

Divorce proceedings of this nature may cost up to $15,000. Lawyers often charge from $150 to $300 an hour for their services. Every telephone conversation is clocked and a record is kept as to how long it takes to type every letter. A charge is made for every minute it takes to drive from one location to another when consultation is going on. On the day they are scheduled to appear in court, the divorcing parties and their lawyers may have to wait three or four hours for their case to be called, and the lawyers are paid for all the hours they wait.

DIVORCE HAS A RIPPLE EFFECT

The day in court simply marks the beginning of another stage that will stretch on, particularly if children are involved. Each child will have to make peace with the divorce again and again as he or she moves through each developmental stage. And even after the youngest child is married and has his or her own home, the parents and the newly married couple will feel the effect of the divorce or be affected by it.

The effect of the divorce ripples out and influences the extended family and friends of the divorcing couple.

"Before the divorce, we were friends of our daughter-in-law's parents," the parents of one divorcing son said. "We belong to the same church; but now when we see them, the father is distant, the mother cold."

"My wife and I had mutual friends," one divorced man said, "but after the divorce some remained my friends only, and some hers, and some dropped their friendship with both of us."

Divorce also affects the financial situation of both. Often both members of the divorced couple struggle to get along with less money than they had before.

DIVORCE CAN CREATE STRESSFUL SITUATIONS

Some divorce settlements can be amicable and relatively free of tension. If children are involved, and disagreements arise about child custody, support, division of property, and visitation, tension builds. Effects of the stress show up everywhere. The quality of work on the job suffers. Weary parents are too tired or busy to give needed attention to the children. Children's grades may plummet, and behavior problems may appear.

Parents of the divorcing couple worry. One mother said:

"Before the divorce was finalized, our daughter's husband would come and urinate on her front door. We worried because we knew he always carried a gun. Once, he snatched the baby and made off with her. The police phoned and said they had the child. The days were one nightmare after another."

"The children became unmanageable," one grandmother said. "When their father was driving the van, they would unbuckle their seat belts and walk around in the van, or they would unlock and try to open a door while he was driving on the freeway."

"We became so uptight those days," a grandfather recalled, "that both of us had minor accidents, and my wife became seriously ill."

Unfortunately, the anger, the desire to retaliate, the bitterness, the self-centeredness, and all the other destructive emotions stirred up during this time may continue to smolder longer and have far more damaging effects on personalities than was ever envisioned at the beginning.

Divorce Is a Grief Experience

There is much to mourn: the loss of the original family structure; the death of dreams for the future of the family, the children, and the grandchildren; the death of relationships; the loss of homes. For the noncustodial parent, there is the death of the experience of living daily in a shared residence with the children and watching them grow up.

"The silence of the house after my wife took the children and moved out was deafening," one father said. "You can't imagine what it's like to go from years with the chatter and movement of children all around you to an empty house. Empty beds. Empty chests of drawers. A few forgotten toys strewn around. Even our dog was gone. I couldn't bear looking at the children's pictures. I turned them toward the wall."

Someone has said divorced couples can expect a year of intense mourning for every five years of marriage. And as long as the son or daughter is grieving, the parents grieve.

FIND SUPPORT

Few of us can make it on our own. Your child will need support, but so will you. Run, don't walk, in your search for help. You'll need listening ears, shoulders to cry on, someone to hug you or take you out to lunch. Someone with whom to pray.

I don't know where you are in this process now. Perhaps you are at the very beginning. Perhaps you are busy assisting a child getting settled in a new home. Perhaps you are five or six years down the road, and problems continue to arise.

We can't begin to discuss all the problems or situations you are facing or will face. But we'll share with you how divorce has impacted us, and then maybe you won't feel so alone. We'll also tell you what has helped us cope. Most of us are grandparents, so we'll talk about that aspect, too. And finally, we'll discuss some of the things we have learned and some of the good things that can come out of divorce.

～ *Chapter Two* ～
Why Has Our Child's Divorce Hit Us So Hard?

The most difficult and painful experience in my husband's and my life has been the divorce of our child. It pained us to see the family we had watched come into formation break up. Our family never had experienced divorce. We had believed, and still believe, in the biblical teaching that supports loving, lasting marriages. We ourselves entered into marriage intending it to last, and we expected our children would do so, too.

Unfortunately, marriages don't always last. Sometimes divorce does become necessary. With easy availability to it, divorce has become common. Still, when the family breaks into pieces, people grieve. The couple, and to some extent the parents of the couple, may feel they failed in one of the most important ventures of a lifetime: the marriage venture.

"The divorce of our son caused much reflection on our part," a father wrote. "We wondered if what we had experienced at home had any influence on how things developed for him. That was painful."

Divorce hits families hard because they have not expected it and may not have experienced it before in their family.

The chronic nature of divorce means the effect of the divorce goes on and on. One father noted that five years had elapsed but the problems continued.

One woman said ruefully, "I'm wondering if we'll ever enjoy good relations with our one granddaughter. We've helped pay college expenses, but we've never received a word of thanks. We've offered to buy a plane ticket so she could come and visit us, but she has never accepted it. I had hoped when she got older she would see things differently."

The reason or cause for the divorce also influences how parents feel about the divorce. If physical cruelty, alcohol or drug abuse, failure to provide for the family, or infidelity, etc., were cited, parents may heave a sigh of relief that the marriage is coming to an end. One mother said she had asked her daughter why it had taken her so long to end the marriage. Another mother admitted she actually had been urging her daughter to end hers.

However, parents who could perceive no justifiable reason why their child had initiated the divorce struggled with feelings of disappointment with the child. One father said he had been a little angry with his son and had told him he should have tried harder.

"Everybody in our family knows *he* isn't easy to live with," he said.

"We were fond of his wife," the mother said. "We didn't want to lose her."

The way in which parents get the news also makes a difference as to how grievously the announcement affects them. Some had received a phone call, others a letter. One couple had already separated before the parents heard of the intent. A number of parents said they hadn't known about the unhappiness in the marriage until their child told them.

"In our case it was our son," one mother said. "He had been unhappy, but he did not initiate the breakup. He sobbed as he told us all about it; and, when a heart is breaking, what can one do to ease the pain? I wish I could forget the evening we learned about it, but I can't."

"My wife was dying," one elderly father said. "One of our daughters, who lives overseas, had come to be with my wife and me, but finally she had to leave. Her husband of thirty-five years met her at the airport and told her he wanted out of the marriage. He was going to marry a woman they had taken into their home to help.

"Our daughter called her sister who was living in the United States. Together they decided that with my wife dying, I had enough to deal with. We had been married sixty-five years. So they didn't tell me until after my wife died. I was shocked, and then I felt doubly bad because I sensed hate in my daughter toward her ex-husband, and that troubled me." He paused.

"It wasn't until several years later when their son, who was living in another country, came to spend a night with his mother that things changed. His father was to come by and pick him up in the morning.

When he came, our daughter invited him in for coffee, and in doing so, the hate she had nursed all these years somehow lost its grip on her. She said it was just gone. I was so relieved and happy. It had been totally uncharacteristic of her to hate."

In another case, the family had just lived through the divorce of a son when the father became critically ill. They rejoiced, however, when a second son came to spend Christmas with them, but joy turned into dismay when he told them he had left his wife. He was doing graduate work and had met and fallen in love with a woman he had met at the university. The parents had known there had been trouble off and on in the marriage. But they had not known the situation was as serious as it had become.

"There's always fault on both sides," the mother said. "Anyway, when this news broke, my husband was dying. He said to me, 'I can't deal with this; you'll have to.' It was very hard."

The length of the child's marriage also contributes to the degree of grief parents feel. One set of parents explained their child had been married only a little over a year, they had met her husband only briefly before the marriage, and the couple lived several thousand miles from them. They said the divorce really hadn't touched them.

Later, however, this couple experienced the divorce of a child who had been married more than thirty years. The children involved were adults by the time of the divorce.

"They had made so much history together," one parent said. "They had a beautiful home—had worked on it together. And then to throw it all overboard—why? We grieved deeply over that divorce."

Concern about the grandchildren deepens the grief of the grandparents.

"When one spouse poisons the minds of the children against the other spouse, as happened in our case, everybody suffers," one parent said. "It's abusing the child to do so. No parent or grandparent should say anything to alienate a child from the other parent. The child has an absolute right to a neutral or positive posture of one parent toward the other no matter how he or she feels about the other. A parent's animosity should not be transferred to the child."

"Our son, who was the noncustodial parent, had become ill and was living with us," one mother said. "His child began to say horrible things, calling him names like 'homeless bum.' We were shocked at the disrespect and the language."

"Our daughter's husband had kept the children from us before the divorce," one mother said. "He was abusive, lazy, and had affairs with other women. We were glad when our daughter finally filed for divorce. She was granted custody. When our daughter first brought the children to us, they were afraid to come into the house or get near us. I gave a little gift to one. She gave it back and later wrote a note that read, 'You're not my grandma. You're mean.' Two years have passed. Things are improving, but this one grandchild still will say hurtful things."

One woman, in speaking about her son's divorce five years ago and subsequent remarriage said, "My son and his second wife are happily married, but I'm not sure how the children feel."

Another said her son had remarried, too, and a child had been born. She said their granddaughter liked her stepmother and was "crazy" about the baby. "What a relief!" she said.

Proximity to the divorcing couple makes a difference in the impact on the parents.

"Our son chose not to involve us. Living several hundred miles away, that was easy," one parent said. "We didn't know his wife well, either, so his divorce scarcely affected us."

On the other hand, another mother said the great distance between them and their daughter had increased their anxiety. "We felt so helpless," she said. "What could we do?"

In two instances, a daughter had shown up on the parents' doorstep and had continued to live with them until after the divorce. The parents had been immersed in all the proceedings. "I hope I don't have to live through that experience again," one said.

Giving financial help may become a difficult issue for parents who get involved, especially in the beginning. In some cases, they gave help in the form of a loan. One child, five years after the divorce, was still making payments. In another instance, the child had asked for and received a loan but was doing nothing to repay it.

Emotional outbursts between their child and themselves cause most parents sadness. Relationships became strained, they said. The child had made hurtful remarks, and then they, the parents, had responded hastily. In addition to their sorrow over the divorce, the parents grieved about the broken relationship with their child.

If parents feel estranged from their child, but don't know why they are feeling that way, answering three questions may help them understand why they are depressed and miserable:

(1) How often does your child enable you to feel loved or cared for?

(2) How often does your child create tension or begin to argue with you?

(3) How often does your child offer to help *you* with some of your chores and responsibilities?

Having answered these questions, each parent needs to find his or her way to handle these frustrations and restore harmony.

Lack of previous experience or making mistakes during the divorce proceedings can leave parents and the child ignorant of their rights or fearful of things they need not fear.

Other factors might cause stress on parents: financial problems and their health, the divorce and remarriage of other children, or a recent transition to retirement. Occasionally the divorce of a child will bring to a head unhappiness in the marriage of the parents that has been covered up or ignored.

A previous strained relationship with a child or child's ex-spouse can set in motion a whole array of conflicting emotions and can prevent reasonable negotiations.

When a divorce takes place, the load for parents who care about their child and their grandchildren can become heavy, and if other factors are added to that load, it can become so heavy that parents wonder how they can go on. They recognize they are being taxed beyond their physical and emotional abilities, perhaps beyond their financial ability if the child's needs are considerable or appear to be long-term, and beyond their ability to know how to act wisely. They also might be feeling they are failing their child because they should be doing more to help, but at the same time they know there is very little, and perhaps nothing, they can do to ease the hurt their child feels.

When parents begin to feel this way, it is time to stop and consider thoughtfully and prayerfully how to cope, because if parents are going to be able to help, they need to be healthy and strong physically, emotionally, and spiritually. We'll discuss that next.

ᗡ Chapter Three ᗡ
Taking Care of Ourselves

To be the most effective helper, we need, first of all, to take care of ourselves. To be strong for another, we need to be strong ourselves. To give, we must have something to give. To take care of ourselves is not selfish, but absolutely necessary. Some suggestions follow.

Maintain Physical and Mental Health

Get plenty of sleep. Exercise. A brisk walk, a swim in the pool, a game of tennis, a vigorous vacuuming of the house, or physical movement of any kind will trigger release of chemicals in our body such as endorphins and serotonin. These reduce stress and improve our sense of well being.

Eat well-balanced meals. Practice beginning every day with fifteen or twenty minutes of quiet time to read, meditate, and pray. Follow that by developing the habit of replacing negative thoughts with positive, faith-filled, hopeful ones. Ask God to help you and your child find opportunities for growth in this experience, painful though it is.

Get Rid of Guilt

When a child announces the intent to divorce, often one of the first thoughts of a parent is, "What did I do wrong?" Probably nothing.

Many forces shape our children outside of the influence of home and family. Friends, the media, and the popular thinking of the day are but a few. After the children move out of the home, parents may know very little about their lives—especially if the children live at a distance. Parents may try to keep in touch by phone calls, e-mail, letters, and visits, but even then their knowledge may be incomplete. As parents, we know this, but when a crisis like divorce strikes, we need friends to remind us of these realities again.

Sometimes specific doubts may trouble us. Talking to a friend can help. One couple, who had served overseas on special assignment, had to send their children away to boarding school. A number of years later when their daughter divorced, feelings of guilt tortured the mother. "Had sending my daughter away from home when she was a child contributed in any way to my daughter's inability to have a good marriage?" she asked.

This question did not trouble the father. "I have always believed," he said, "that although we have made mistakes as parents, we did the best we knew how."

Parents who can say this have an easier time adjusting to changed situations that take place in their children's lives. But if a parent continues to feel guilty, discussing this openly may help. If indeed her daughter feels that leaving home while she was young made life difficult for her, the mother may share her sorrow, apologize for any harm caused unwittingly, and ask for forgiveness. Hopefully the daughter will grant it. Even if she doesn't, the mother then may place the matter in God's hands and leave it there.

TRY TO UNDERSTAND
WHY THE DIVORCE HAPPENED

When a divorce takes place, most, if not all, parents try and reason out why the divorce "happened." So the parents, and often the family, talk together. They recall the past: dating days, marriage, early years of marriage, remarks made, incidents that happened, and the behavior of both. Some tell about noticing (and ignoring) indications of a crumbling relationship. In some instances, the one getting divorced opens up and tells things the family has not heard before. As the talks continue, usually a picture begins to emerge. Sometimes the family reaches conclusions that satisfy them. Then they can more readily accept the divorce.

"She was a high energy person; he was laid-back," they say. "They married too young. They married with romantic ideas in mind and did not understand what it means to love." "He was extremely frugal; she wanted to have a nice home." "She always had to be in control; he found this oppressive." "I think he had a mid-life crisis. They had been married twenty-three years. Our daughter was very involved with her children, teaching, friends, home, and garden. Perhaps he felt he needed more attention than she gave him."

At the same time, parents acknowledge there is always her story and his story and someplace in the

middle is the true story, which they may never discover or understand. Not knowing the story fully, can
evaluations be accurate?

TAKE TIME TO GRIEVE

Grieving is a coping mechanism. Let the tears flow.
Feel the pain. How intense and how prolonged your
grief will be will depend on your proximity to your
child, the extent to which your child shares his or her
grief with you, and how well your child is adjusting
and moving on to create a new life. If grandchildren
are involved, you will grieve if you see indications of
inability to adjust and accept.

Undoubtedly you have lived through the loss of
one or more significant ones in your life, and so
grief is not an uncharted experience for you. You
know something about denial, anger, depression,
lack of energy, irritability, and all the other disturb-
ing emotions that accompany grieving, so when
these emotions surface now, you will recognize
them for what they are.

A grandfather who has lived through several
divorces in his family said, "I felt my daughter's hurt.
She was hurting so much. There was nothing I could
do." Speaking about his granddaughter's divorce, he
said, "I felt so helpless. I was so sad. I hurt so much."

SUPPORT GROUPS

Support groups aren't for everybody, but I personally
have found them helpful. Being with others who listen and understand because they've been where I am

now relieves the loneliness. I am able to unload some of my pain. If tears come, I can let them flow, and talking about my situation sometimes clarifies things for me. In support groups, I can listen to others and borrow their ideas. Perhaps most importantly, the support group I am in knows how to "take it to the Lord in prayer."

If you are not in a support group, don't know where to find one, or don't feel comfortable in a group, find someone to whom you can talk. Do this especially if your spouse has died. The load is too heavy to bear by yourself.

Eliminate Stress Factors If You Can

The process of divorce takes time. As the days and weeks of waiting pass, stress may build for parents. They long for relief. Take the time to step back and look at the list of stress-building factors noted in the previous chapter and ask if there are things that can change. Some things can't be changed. "I never fight things I can't change," one wise father said.

But sometimes parents can do something to lessen tension. When two parents found that their son, upset over the divorce, had become argumentative, they learned not to ask intrusive questions that he might resent and about which he would begin to argue.

One father felt his daughter was asking her mother to babysit too often. "I had lost my wife," he said. "She never had time to go places or do things with me."

He finally asked all three to sit down and talk. Boundaries were defined. As they were observed, harmony in the family returned.

KNOW YOUR LIMITATIONS

Sometimes it is appropriate to say "no." Not all parents will want to care for children. Not all parents are willing to see life savings depleted.

SEE THE DIVORCE IN PERSPECTIVE

One mother told of how often she would break down and cry when talking to one of her daughters. One day when this happened, the daughter interrupted her and said, "But Mom, you have three other children who are all doing great and having no problems. Doesn't this mean anything to you?"

"I saw in a flash," the mother said, "that I had been letting the divorce situation of our one child fill the whole picture. I deliberately started that day to give thanks for all the good things that are ours. My depression began to lift, and I stopped crying."

As time moves on, we may discover that our child has much to give us.

"I'm so proud of the person my daughter has become," one mother said.

All the members of my group spoke with appreciation of support from their families and friends. Siblings of the divorced child called both the parents and their sibling frequently. Some came for brief visits when parents or the divorcing child needed them.

"It was beautiful to see the children caring for each other," one mother said.

"I was both humbled and gratified," another mother said, "when friends would write to say they were praying for us daily."

A father told of his dismay when his son agreed to some provisions in the divorce he thought were unfair to him. "But I was helpless," he said, "and so after thinking long about it, I decided instead to rejoice in his loving, forgiving, generous spirit."

BECOME INFORMED

Read. Understanding the legal process helps to alleviate fears.

One mother said she found help in talking with other parents whose children had divorced.

Accept the fact that family members may disagree about certain issues. A father said that during the time of waiting, he and his wife disagreed, argued, and even had been quite angry with each other. The mother hastened to add that they always talked things out and they always were in agreement that they would do all they could to support their child.

UNDERSTAND THE CUSTODY ARRANGEMENTS

Even when physical custody is awarded to the mother, divorce papers often make it clear that legal custody belongs to both. At the very least this means father and mother meet regularly and discuss and plan for the future of the children. Unilateral planning is discouraged. Unfortunately, sometimes this stipulation is not observed.

Today, many parents are requesting—and judges are awarding—joint custody of the children. In order for the award to be of more than a psychological benefit to the father, an amicable separation is necessary so the other parent will cooperate fully.

For joint custody to work, it is best if the two parents live in close proximity. Then, regardless of which home the children live in, they can continue to attend the same school and play with the same friends. This assumes that both father and mother have dwelling places large enough to accommodate the children.

Two of the parents told of such an arrangement, with the grandchildren in one home three days of the week and four in the other. The following week the order is reversed. The arrangement seemed to be working out with the exception that children frequently want some item that has been left in the other home. In these two situations, birthdays and holidays are celebrated jointly. So far, no remarriages have taken place.

In another case, the son lived with his father a certain number of years, then went to live with his mother. In another instance when the mother moved to another city, the children lived with her during the school year and spent summers and long holidays with their father.

"Why shouldn't the responsibilities and joys be shared?" one divorced mother asked. "The children need fathers as much as mothers. And the children are the father's children as much as the mother's."

Asked how the children under joint custody were faring, one grandmother said, "From all we can judge, so far the children appear happy and untroubled. They are eight and eleven years old now. Who knows what they will say when they become adults?"

If custodial arrangements can be made that please both parents, it will be a lot easier for the grandparents.

Sometimes, however, relationships between the divorcing father and mother continue to be hostile, and fathers are consigned to the position of noncustodial "visiting fathers" only. Many fathers grieve over this situation.

"I feel," said one, "as though I am locked in a cage; and when my ex-wife comes along with a key and lets me out, I have a brief time to see the children. Then I'm put in the cage again and shut away from the children. Others have access to the children, but I don't, even if I am their father."

"Every time I take the children back to their mother and say goodbye to them, it's like a knife pierces me," another father said.

So intense is the pain of separation for some of the noncustodial "visiting fathers" that studies have shown they simply disappear or stop visiting the children. Frequently when visitation stops, child support also stops.

In situations like this, grandparents grieve. They have to come to terms with the fact that there is much parents cannot do. They cannot legislate custody arrangements. They cannot take away another's pain. They cannot hasten the healing process. They cannot make people forgive each other. To relieve their frustration, parents need to seek refreshing and renewing experiences: listening to music, gardening, doing crossword puzzles, shopping, lunch with friends. Each person's list is different. One mother said being called back to work was wonderful therapy. The most frequently mentioned source of help was prayer. Prayer puts us in touch with God, who is ready to quicken hope when hope dims. God will act in us, through us, and for us.

Take care of yourself. Remember, no one else can do it for you. Only you can.

⁓ Chapter Four ⁓
Ways Parents Can Help

When children marry, their parents usually step back and encourage the couple to establish their own home and build their own lives. However, when a divorce occurs, roles often reverse. Society has provided parents with no specific guidelines, and so parents try to meet each situation as it presents itself. Parents, it appears, fall into four categories.

The first group says, "Our child is an adult. Let our child figure out what to do." These parents have no involvement in the situation. The second group says to a child, "Let us know if you need help," and then they wait for the child to ask. The third group lends a listening ear; as the parents listen, they perceive apparent needs and offer help. The fourth group of parents immerse themselves in the life of their child and often feel they have never done enough. Parents who live near their child probably will be involved in giving more help, and when parents and child live together, needs will be most obvious of all.

"Help when help is needed, but don't infantilize," one parent cautioned.

Types of Parental Support
Advice
Most parents said they hesitated to give advice lest it rob the child of the responsibility of making his or

her own decisions and living with the conse-
quences. However, not to give advice except when
asked calls for great self-restraint, faith in the child,
and wise love.

"If you feel strongly that you must say something," one said, "say it in a sentence, not in a
paragraph."

"I suggested to our daughter that she join a support group," one mother said. "She went two or three
times and then said, 'That's not for me,' and quit. I
think she could have been helped by continuing;
when she chose not to, there was nothing I could do."

As parents, we need to be flexible and allow our
child to be different from us.

One parent said she tried to help her child see what
mistakes had been made so she wouldn't repeat them.
She believes our task as parents is to help our children
understand what their choices entail and how the
choices will affect their lives in the future.

Another parent said she and her husband
encouraged their child to cultivate and maintain
amicable relations with the ex-spouse, knowing that
indirectly this would benefit their children. They
were careful not to say anything negative about the
absent parent and urged their child to speak respect-
fully about the ex-spouse. If child support payments
were late, the parents urged their child to seek a solu-
tion by meeting with the ex-spouse and a mediator
rather than engaging a lawyer to press the case. They
said they understood how costly this can become and
how relationships are likely to deteriorate even more.

Networking
Sometimes parents can suggest resources in the community that can provide needed help to the child. Is the child looking for an affordable apartment? Does the newly divorced mother need training so she can get a job later? Is she trained already but needs employment? Does the mother need to find a reliable child care center? Parents sometimes know people who can help.

Emotional support
The most common type of emotional support is thoughtful, sympathetic listening, as we let our child know that we care for, love unconditionally, value, and esteem him or her. One parent said he tried to avoid remarks that might make his son feel sorry for himself, and instead they encouraged him to accept the challenge before him.

One couple said they hoped they could be a stable element in the lives of their grandchildren when everything else seemed to be crumbling.

Financial aid
While a few parents said the divorce had not cost them anything financially, many others had given aid, some considerably. The divorced child needed money to help make mortgage payments, pay attorney fees, and for taxes, among other things. In one instance, the parents made a down payment on a townhouse and paid the monthly mortgage fees until their daughter was able to assume them. In another

instance, the parents bought a car so their daughter could get to work.

Housing and hospitality

A number of parents had given shelter for varying lengths of time, in one instance for four months and later for six months.

In one case, primary custody of the children was given to the father, whose job occasionally took him away from the city. He shared this problem in conversation with his parents who lived several hundred miles away. The parents talked it over and decided to take early retirement and move to the city where their son lived. He invited them to live with him. The grandfather found part-time work, and the grandmother took over the care of the house and the children.

One noncustodial father likes the warmth, space, and play opportunities for the children at his parent's home, and so he brings them there regularly.

Child care

"I care for our daughter's child when she is working," one mother said. "Yes, it has meant curtailing social activities and rearranging my schedule, but I had been so worried about both my daughter's and granddaughter's safety before, that I've been glad to help."

Needs of the children

One grandmother told that her grandson had needed glasses. She offered to pay half the cost, and he got his glasses. "But I don't limit my help to our divorced child," she said. "Our other daughter had heavy car expenses. I sent a check so they could have a happy Christmas."

Household tasks
One grandmother spends one day a week in her daughter's home, cleaning and doing laundry. A grandfather is on call to repair things that break. Two parents traveled several hundred miles to paint their daughter's new apartment. They return periodically to make needed repairs or help in whatever way they can.

Household furnishings
Another couple paid for the furniture for an apartment. Because giving help is such a "sticky" issue, parents and child do well to think carefully before they give help. Raeann R. Hamon in her article, "Parents as Resources When Adult Children Divorce," (published in the *Journal of Divorce and Remarriage,* Vol. 23 [1/2], 1995), suggests a few questions to consider.

She asks how support from parents will affect the divorced child as he or she adjusts to living as a single person. She wonders what it will cost children to receive support, and what are the rewards. Then she ponders how parents and children together can arrive at a mutual agreement as to what help is appropriate and helpful and will be appreciated. Her last question deserves attention as the impact of divorce continues year after year. The support parents extend during the first couple of years after a divorce may not be the wisest to continue indefinitely. How long should help continue?

Two divorced mothers told about some of the help they had received and what it had meant to them. Here is what they wrote:

> In my divorce, some things were easy. It was pretty clear that I did not have to justify my reasons. It's been said if a spouse engages in any of the three A's—adultery, abuse, or addiction—a divorce need not be questioned. I had suffered all three.
>
> I had a good job so I needed no financial assistance, but I needed friends and family to "complain to," and on whose shoulders I could cry. My biggest worry was my then two-year-old child. Because of my twenty-four-hour shifts as a fire fighter/paramedic, conventional daycare was not an option. My parents rose to the occasion and have helped raise a bright, caring, well-rounded child who is now eleven. Two to three days a week, while she was with them, I knew she would be well fed, well rested, and well loved. I'll never forget when my dad said, "I really miss Kacee when she's not here. I get up every night to use the bathroom and always check to make sure she's covered up—and forget when she's not here."
>
> My daughter has learned so much from her grandparents: how to ride a bike, multiply fractions, bake bread, and something I couldn't teach her: how you can make a marriage work for more than fifty years.
>
> —Janet

Without my family's support, I don't believe I would have made it through this difficult time. Even though I knew in my heart that my marriage was a disaster, I resisted their help for a while. But fortunately they persisted. My mother gave me both emotional and financial support, accompanied me on my initial trip to the attorney, and helped me out in whatever way she could. My siblings also were there to support me. And my family is still there, even after the "crazy time."

—Laurie

∽ Chapter Five ∽
Grandparents and Their Grandchildren

Grandchildren are special, and a unique relationship develops between grandchildren and grandparents. Grandparents take pleasure in them, indulge them, and love them. When a divorce threatens, grandchildren and their futures suddenly come to the fore of grandparent's attention and concern.

Grandparents wonder what life will be like now for the children. Will they experience hardship? What will life be like for them growing up without their own father or mother in the home? What will their life be like if they are raised by a stepparent? And what will life be like for them as grandparents? Will they see the grandkids as often as they wish?

Grandparents' dilemma

Sam and Janet faced these questions when their daughter arrived home with her children. What could the Sam and Janet do but take them in? Suddenly the grandparents' peaceful retired life vanished. The house shrank in size as the volume of noise increased. Breakfasts, dinners, evenings—everything changed.

Their daughter was often visibly upset and distracted. One night, after the children were in bed, she talked with her parents about the future she faces. Their talk was interrupted by one of the children who crawled out of bed and came into the living room. "I can't sleep," he said.

On the other side of town, the child's father sat alone, missing the children tremendously. His parents came just to be with him, not knowing what else to do. They too wondered about the grandchildren. Would they be able to see them as often as they wished? What would the future be like for their son? They too are hurting.

Within the next months—perhaps a year or more—some form of new life will begin to take shape for all of them. Sam and Janet's daughter's stay at home may be temporary. If it becomes permanent, the daughter will lose some of the privacy and autonomy she knew before, and so will her parents. If her work takes her away from home for many hours, the grandparents will have to become surrogate parents, a role they many not enjoy as much as being grandparents. Differences of opinion may arise. At times the older parents may think their daughter is too lenient, at other times too strict. If their daughter decides to move out and rent a place of her own, the parents worry about how she will pay the rent, the utilities, the bills for the car. The anxieties go on and on.

Across town, the other grandparents tried to do what they know will help them see their grandchildren as often as they wish. They are experienced enough in life so when trouble first began, they said, "There's fault on both sides." But it's natural that they take the side of their own child. Staying on friendly terms with their son's ex-wife was not easy.

One morning when the grandchildren were in school, Janet thought about the many friends she knew who had children who had divorced. Gudrun had worked so hard to help her daughter-in-law and the grandchildren after the divorce, and now the daughter-in-law was trying to prevent the children's father from visiting them. After Claudia's daughter and son-in-law were divorced, both of them remarried—and their new spouses already had children. So Claudia was now trying to cope with two large blended families. And then there was Rita. What a shock Rita had when her son told her he was gay, and his wife was really a lesbian; the two had decided to get married only because they each wanted a child. Once married, they hadn't been able to tolerate one another, so they divorced. And now her son had found a male partner, and they had applied to adopt a child.

"Life has become so complicated!" Janet thought. "If only all these divorces didn't affect the innocent children so much. So many questions. So many problems."

Perhaps the most complicated situation arises when families are blended. In today's world the recoupling patterns of divorce and remarriage that can affect grandparents are too numerous to consider in this small book. Perhaps the wisest general advice is: consult with all the parents involved, strive for family cohesiveness, and try to be sensitive to everyone's emotions.

It is sad and stressful when an unfriendly custodial parent does not allow the grandchildren to visit
their grandparents. In the past, courts have not
granted visitation rights to grandparents, but in
recent years some grandparents have worked with
lawyers who specialize in grandparent rights to bring
the matter before the courts. Results are mixed. Even
if the judge awards visitation rights to the grandparents, a hostile attitude from a custodial parent may so
influence the children that the visits may be unpleas-
ant for the grandparents.

How grandchildren feel
The weeks and months preceding the actual
divorce are very difficult for the children. The
world has become an unsafe place for them. They
feel insecure. Will they be abandoned? Will they be
put in foster homes? Will they be able to go to college now that this has happened?

Children worry. A few weeks after their mother
had taken the children and moved back to her parent's home, the three-year-old daughter was spending
an afternoon with her dad. She crawled up in his lap.

"I think of you all alone here in the house," she
said. "You must be very lonely." And then seeing the
tears that were rolling down his cheeks, she kissed
him, brushed away his tears, and asked, "Would it
help if we went riding bikes together?"

Her one-year-old sister was confused. When her
dad brought her back after an afternoon of visiting,
she would cling to him. When he loosened her arms

from around his neck and put her down on the floor, she would wrap her arms around his leg. When the door was shut between them, she would stand at the screen door with her face flattened against the screen, watching her father drive away. What emotions were tearing at her that she could not understand or put in words?

Children of divorce need a lot of reassurance, a lot of loving. Children are reacting to the many changes over which they have no control, beginning with the break-up of the family.

"Can't you fix things?" a nine-year-old begged his dad.

It's especially hard on the children when their parents begin to date other people. One day when they are in the mall, the children might see their dad with another woman. Or one of the parents may say sarcastic things about the other or try to win their loyalty. This troubles the children and upsets them. They love both their mom and dad. They feel pulled this way and that. They may feel lonely if they refuse to take sides.

Divorce is also a time of feeling guilty. The children might wonder what they did to cause the break-up. Some may become extraordinarily well-behaved to make up for previous mistakes.

Divorce is a time of sadness and yearning for the children. "I wish we all could be together like a family," children may say. Or "Don't you think Mom and Dad will get together again? Can't we pray for this?"

Thoughtful children, though perhaps unconsciously, try to do what their elders are trying to do, which is to come to a cognitive acceptance of the divorce. Two years after his parent's divorce, a nine-year-old said, "It's all right, I guess. I try to think of it this way. I say to myself, 'Dad's away working; and when he can get time off, he'll come and get me, and we'll be together again until he has to go to work.'" He paused. Then he added, "But it was best when we all lived together."

His older brother, whose frustration sometimes broke out in destructive behavior, burst out, "I don't want to belong to a divorced family!" There were tears in his eyes as he said it.

Children may chew clothing or bite their lips when they have trouble facing their emotions. Some may whine and cling to their parents. Occasionally, children may have temper tantrums, pick fights, and hit each other (or even adults). It isn't uncommon for this sort of anger to be directed at their father.

During this tempestuous time, grandparents will discover, sooner or later, that when the children come for a visit—and especially an extended one—they have to set limits, mark out boundaries, hold kids responsible for what they do, make a few rules, and discipline them. Wise grandparents learn to set as few rules as possible. Having too many means the children will ignore them all. Grandchildren now grown said they would have liked, when they were little, to have been allowed to set some of the rules together with their parents and grandparents. Differences in generations can complicate the situation. What Grandma considers intolerable, her daughter or son accepts.

It takes a long time before children accept and adapt to their new roles and places and start to feel secure and peaceful. As everyone adjusts, grandparents may find little joy in visits with their grandchildren. They may struggle to find things to talk about or do with their grandchildren.

One grandchild, now a young adult, added that grandparents shouldn't feel hurt if the grandchildren did fewer things with them when they became adolescents. The grandchildren still loved the grandparents as much as ever, he said; they, as children, were only trying to grow up. Another grandchild said they understood when grandparents were too old to run or play ball; they wished they could, but they understood.

Being grandparents to children of divorced homes is an assignment calling for much thought, planning, patience, understanding, and love.

"But it has its rewards," one grandmother said. "Our two grandchildren, who were hostile at first, are loving and responsive now. That makes up for all the difficult days we lived through."

Are there any other rewards for parents whose son or daughter divorces? Can any good come out of divorce? We'll talk about that in the next chapter.

∽ Chapter Six ∽

Can Any Good
Come out of Divorce?

Many divorces, especially if the proceedings have been hurtful, leave resentment, anger, and a host of uncharitable emotions. It's hard to forgive someone who leaves you for someone else. Noncustodial parents feel robbed of their right to enjoy the daily companionship of their children and watch them grow. Custodial parents may become acrimonious because they have to work so hard. Many situations leave bitterness in their wake.

Laurene Johnson relates her story in her book, *Divorced Kids.* On the sixteenth anniversary of their marriage, her husband, Larry, told her he wanted a divorce. Their children were a twelve-year-old son and an eight-year-old son.

The announcement caught Laurene completely unprepared. After shock and numbness came depression. Anger and resentment simmered within her, too. At the same time, she knew that if the children were to be relatively problem-free and well adjusted, it was important that she recover in a healthy, wholesome way.

Then one day she picked up a book and read how God had endowed her with powers to meet any challenge. Resolve built within her to realize the potential God had planted within her. She admits it took time—lots of time—to grieve and to build up self-esteem. Then eight years after the divorce, her son invited his father and his new wife to Thanksgiving.

Laurene and her ex-husband had been married sixteen years. She had heard someone say it takes half as long for the survivor to heal as the marriage was long. With a little start she realized she was at the halfway mark.

The children were excited. They eagerly awaited the day. When she first greeted her ex-husband and his wife, Laurene felt fluttering in her stomach, but then she was surprised because of the ease with which they all began conversing.

At the table, Brian led in prayer and, among other things, thanked God for the gift of forgiveness. As they ate, Laurene said she realized that somehow she had been able to release her ex-husband from any obligations she felt he owed her.

Later at their son's graduation, the two stood together, Laurene and her ex-husband. Laurene took a step to her right, put an arm around his waist, looked up at him, and said, "Well, we did it." He bent down and said, "Good job, Mom."

Sometimes not only the divorced couple, but also the parents of the couple, need to learn to forgive. If they believe their child has been wronged, the parents will burn with resentment, indignation, and anger.

In his book *The Art of Forgiving,* Lewis B. Smedes writes that in order to forgive, first we must learn to see again the one who has wounded us as a human being, one like us with good points as well as faults and weaknesses. Next we have to let go of what we feel is our right: to get even. When times get tough for the one who has hurt us and our child, we learn to wish for good things instead of saying, "Serves him or her right!"

Praying that God will bless our ex-son-in-law or ex-daughter-in-law is a good place to begin. Instead of praying that God will do something specific to change the other person, we simply ask God to bless him or her. This isn't easy, but it's a first step toward forgiving. As we continue to pray, we shall discover we are beginning to love the person with a different love than we knew before.

Learning to forgive takes time. Sometimes it appears to be an "on again/off again" occurrence. We think we have forgiven and then something pops up that makes us furious again, and we have to go back to point one and start all over again. Eventually, however, we can truly forgive.

Learning to forgive is one of the good things that comes out of divorce. Are there others?

I asked some of the members of the group I interviewed if they could see any good that had resulted from their child's divorce. Here are some of their answers.

"Our daughter had suffered verbal and physical abuse. We were relieved after the divorce took place because we had feared for her safety. She surely has a much better life now."

"Our ex-son-in-law had driven a wedge between us and our daughter. With him out of the way, our relationship to our daughter blossomed and grew."

A father wrote, "Divorce in our family has made me a more tolerant person. At first we were upset and felt judgmental toward our son, but then we came to realize we must accept our son as he is. This was an emotional and also a spiritual journey. It made me ponder the meaning of unconditional love and how that should be applied in our particular case."

One mother said, "I'm so proud of our daughter and so grateful to see how she has become a strong, resourceful, yet compassionate person. I experience so much joy when I am with her."

One mother said that she always had known that in some cases divorce was advisable, but after their child's divorce she became more open to learning how often it is true.

A number indicated their personal spiritual life had been enhanced.

One couple said they saw their grandchildren much more frequently now because previously the children's mother had not encouraged visitation, but now the children's father brought them by often.

Another couple said that they had been drawn closer to each other, and they prized the love they had for each other more than ever.

As has been mentioned, forgiveness can bring freedom and joy. But what if forgiveness is asked and not granted?

"We grieved," two parents wrote, "when our son told his story. In a meeting with his wife before the actual divorce took place, our son said he tried to tell his story, and then he told her he was sorry for any and every way he had hurt her. He told her he still loved her and with tears pleaded with her. Her response was to get up and walk out. The next day she sent him word that she did not want to see him again. Our son pleaded that the two go for counseling together. His wife refused. Our son was crushed."

The mother went on to tell of how he found refuge in prayer: "Though he is Protestant, he noticed a Catholic church nearby that offered early morning mass. As he prayed and received the Sacrament, there was the assurance that *God* had forgiven him for whatever wrong he had done."

"I have tried to forgive," the mother wrote, "but I'm not sure I've succeeded yet. My son still grieves for his children. Will that suffering ever be eased?"

To varying degrees, children from divorced homes experience chronic grief, too, even though they may not be able to identify their feelings as grief. Studies have been made of some divorced families, some five years after the divorce, some after an even longer period of time.

By this time, it is thought, life should have settled down. On average, eighty percent of the men and seventy-five percent of the women have remarried.

Parents and children were asked if a more satisfying family life had come into being because of the divorce. Were the family members happier than before, still unhappy, or no happier than before? All were asked to consider both what had been gained and what had been lost. The directors of the research said if the answer given was "yes, they were happier," the divorce could be considered a success. If the answer was "no" or "questionable," the divorce had failed.

Almost all the divorced adults answered "yes" to the questions, but almost without exception, the children answered "no." Even in those instances, where custody of the children had been shared and the separated parents had homes close enough so the children had been able to attend the same school, the children still wished the family could have remained intact. Well-meaning adults had spoken enthusiastically to the children about how fortunate they had been to have two homes and enlarged families. The children said they would have preferred not having to move from home to home, often missing something that was in the other home and never being able to consider one room of theirs or one entire house as "home."

Those who had been limited to seeing their fathers (often it is the father) only occasionally— weekends or summers—talked about how weary they used to be traveling distances every other week- end. Often they couldn't participate in school events because of their broken schedules. They emphasized that they wanted to be with their father—that wasn't the question—they only wished he could have been with them in the home.

But what if the marriage had been a mistake or a failure and living together would have been impossible? Adult children are able to see the advisability or even the necessity of the divorce. In fact, in some instances when a couple, though unhappy and not enjoying a marriage relationship, have continued to live together until the children are grown and out of the home, some children have said they wish their parents had not done so merely for their sakes. They unselfishly wish their parents could have been happy years earlier even if it had meant a different life for them. They speak now from an adult perspective, not a child's.

Does good come out of divorce? Yes. How much, what kind, and for whom? Does it justify the divorce? Each member of a divorced couple has to answer that for herself or himself.

For those of us who are parents, it is better that we focus on the positive aspects of divorce. Divorce presents us with opportunities to grow, to learn more about healthy relationships, and how to live with and manage power, anxiety, frustration, loss, and grief. The value we place on love, commitments, and freedom can be enhanced. Even if either we or our child feel we have failed in one way or another, God stands ready to meet us at our place of failure. God desires to give us a vision of a life beyond that failure and the resolve, courage, and persistence to aim for a better future. God will go with us every step of the way. Let us trust God.

"The Lord will fulfill his purpose for me;
your steadfast love, O Lord, endures forever,
Do not forsake the work of your hands."
  —Psalm 138:8

Suggested Reading

Johnson, Laurene. *Divorced Kids* (Nashville, Tenn.: T. Nelson, 1990).

Kaslow, Florence W., and Lita Linzer Schwartz. *The Dynamics of Divorce: A Life Cycle Perspective* (Levittown, Pa: Bruner/Mazel, 1987).

McKay, Matthew, Peter D. Rogers, Joan Blades, and Richard Gosse. *The Divorce Book* (Oakland, Calif.: New Harbinger Publications, 1984).

Smedes, Lewis B. *The Art of Forgiving* (Nashville, Tenn.: Moorings, A Division of the Ballantine Publishing Group, Random House, Inc. 1996).

Stewart, Abigail, and Anne P. Copeland, et. al. *Separating Together: How Divorce Transforms Families* (New York: Guildord Press, 1997).

Wallerstein, Judith S., and Joan Berlin Kelly. *Surviving the Break-up: How Children and Parents Cope with Divorce* (New York: Basic Books, Inc. 1980).